CONTENTS

KW-479-019

THE FIVE SENSES

Your five senses tell you what is going on around you. Do you know what they are?

When Jack eats an orange, he uses all his **five senses**.

He **sees** the shape and colour of the orange.

He **hears** the munching sound he makes as he chews.

He **feels** the shape of the orange and the roughness of its skin.

He can **smell** the orange.

He can **taste** its sweet juice.

 TRY IT OUT!

Eat a piece of fruit that you like.
Use all your senses!
What can you see, hear, feel, smell and taste?

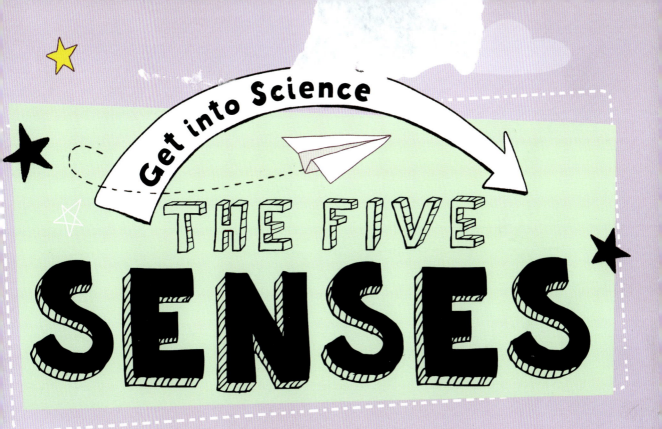

Get into Science

THE FIVE SENSES

Jane Lacey and Sernur Isik

W

Franklin Watts
First published in Great Britain in 2020 by The Watts Publishing Group

Copyright © The Watts Publishing Group, 2020

Credits
Design and project management: Raspberry Books
Art Direction: Sidonie Beresford-Browne
Designer: Kathryn Davies
Consultant: Sally Nankivell-Aston
Illustrations: Sernur Isik

HB ISBN: 978 1 4451 7020 6
PB ISBN: 978 1 4451 7021 3

Printed in Dubai

MIX
Paper from
responsible sources
FSC
www.fsc.org
FSC® C104740

Franklin Watts
An imprint of
Hachette Children's Group
Part of The Watts Publishing Group
Carmelite House
50 Victoria Embankment
London EC4Y 0DZ

An Hachette UK Company
www.hachette.co.uk

www.franklinwatts.co.uk

Different parts of your body send messages to your brain so that you can understand what you are seeing, hearing, feeling, smelling and tasting.

You **see** with your **eyes**.

You **smell** with your **nose**.

You **hear** with your **ears**.

You **taste** with your **tongue**.

You **feel** with your **skin**.

💡 **THINK ABOUT IT!**

Are you using all your senses to read this book? Which ones are you using?

SEEING

You see when you open your eyes and let light into them. What can you see when you shut your eyes and keep out the light?

You **see** colours, shapes and moving things with your **eyes**.

What shapes and colours can you see on this page? Is there anything you have never seen before?

 TRY IT OUT!

Choose one of the things you can see in the picture. Try drawing and colouring it. Be careful to copy the colour and shape.

These two pictures are of the same place, but one shows daytime and the other shows dusk (when it is getting dark).

Which one is the most colourful?

Your eyes can only see colour well in the light.

Animals that go out at night **see much better in the dark** than we do, but their eyes cannot see colour very well. A cat sees things mostly in **black and white**.

 TRY IT OUT!

Shut the curtain in your bedroom in the daytime, but let in a crack of light.
How much colour can you see?
Now open the curtains. How much colour can you see now?

TWO EYES

Having two eyes at the front of your head helps you to work out exactly how near or how far away things are.

🖐 TRY IT OUT!

Hold a pen out in front of you in one hand and the lid in the other hand. Shut one eye and try putting the lid on the pen. Now open both eyes and try again. Is it easier with one eye open or two?

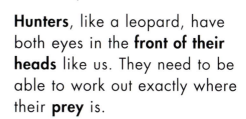

Hunters, like a leopard, have both eyes in the **front of their heads** like us. They need to be able to work out exactly where their **prey** is.

This **antelope** might be the leopard's next meal. Its eyes are on the **side of its head**, which means it can **see all around**. It will quickly spot an enemy like the leopard and try to run away – before it is too late!

🖐 TRY IT OUT!

This bird's eyes are on the side of its head. What animals might it be watching out for? When you look at pictures of animals, notice the size, shape and position of their eyes and think about why they are like that.

HEARING

The sounds you hear with your ears can give you a lot of information about things you may not be able to see. Imagine the sounds that are made by spinning a coin, stirring tea and cutting paper.

TRY IT OUT!

Get some friends to shut their eyes while you make some sounds like the ones in the picture. Ask them to tell you what they are hearing.

Many animals use their sense of hearing to help to **keep them safe**.

A **rabbit** pricks up its ears and **listens out for danger**. It warns the other rabbits to run for cover by thumping its back leg on the ground. All kinds of animals prick up their ears to hear better.

You cannot prick up your ears like a rabbit, but try **cupping your ears** towards a sound like a radio playing softly. It makes a sound easier to hear.

🐞 LOOK AGAIN!

Look again at page 9. Can you see an animal that has eyes on the sides of its head and ears to hear all around that help tell it that an enemy is nearby?

LISTEN to THIS!

One of the most important ways we use our sense of hearing is to listen to what people are saying.

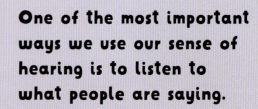

You might listen to a story being **read to you** or your teacher telling you something new. Sometimes you might just enjoy **chatting**.

Animals use sounds to send **messages** to each other, too.

Lambs bleat when they need to find their mothers. Their mothers call 'baa!' back.

Whales sing out strange noises to each other under water.

12

THINK ABOUT IT!

Can you remember any of things that have been said to you today? Were any of them important messages?

You can use your eyes as well as your ears to work out what people are telling you.

People who **cannot hear** use their eyes instead of their ears to understand what people are saying to them. They **use sign language** and can also tell what people are saying by watching their lips move.

THINK ABOUT IT!

When you listen to someone speaking to you, where do you look? Do you understand better if you look at the person speaking to you?

TRY IT OUT!

Without making a sound, try asking a friend to come to your house to play. Now tell them silently that you are hungry and want something to eat.

TOUCH

You can tell a lot about something just by touching it. When you touch something, you feel what it is like.

Imagine **feeling** the hairbrush in this picture with your eyes shut. You would quickly guess what it was because you have seen and felt a hairbrush before.

 TRY IT OUT!

Ask a friend to put some objects into a pillow case, including something that you have never seen before. Make sure that there are no sharp edges or points. Try to guess what the objects are just by feeling them. Which ones are easy to guess and which ones are difficult?

Your **skin** is the part of your body that you feel with. The skin on your **fingertips** is very sensitive to touch so they are very good for feeling things.

 **TRY IT OUT!**

Ask a friend to shut her eyes. Touch both points of a hair grip on the back her hand. How many points can she feel? Touch the points on her fingertips. How many points can she feel now? Which is more sensitive, the skin on her fingertips or the skin on the back of her hands?

 **LOOK AGAIN!**

Look again at page 4. What does Jack feel with his fingers?

FEELERS

Animals feel things with their skin like you do, but they have other ways of feeling things, too.

Have you ever played blindman's buff or put out your hands to feel what is around you to stop yourself bumping into something in the dark?

Whiskers work in rather the same way. They help mice to **feel** what is going on all around them in the dark.

🐾 LOOK AGAIN!

Look again at page 7. How do you think the cat's whiskers help it to hunt?

Snails have feelers on top of their heads called **antennae**. The antennae reach out and feel if something is in the way before the snail bumps into it.

Insects have amazing **antennae**, which they use to touch and feel things. They also use their antennae o smell and to help them balance!

THINK ABOUT IT!

How many other animals can you think of that have whiskers or antennae? Why do you think antennae are sometimes called feelers?

SMELL

You can't see smells, but they are all around you in the air you breathe. The part of your body that senses smell is right up inside your nose – so you smell better if you give a good sniff!

Most things have some kind of smell. **Have you smelled any of these before?**

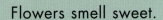

Flowers smell sweet.

Your favourite food smells delicious.

A dirty dish cloth smells disgusting.

TRY IT OUT!

Ask an adult to help you to choose some things with a strong smell, like a lemon, some soap or a shoe. See if a friend can guess what the objects are without seeing or touching them – just by sniffing. Don't sniff powders like flour or talc as they can get up your nose and damage it.

Smells often give important **messages**.

The sweet smell of a flower tells a bee that there is food to eat.

The **bad** smell of a dish cloth warns you that it is full of germs. You know it is time to find a clean one.

Fresh food smells **good** and makes you feel hungry and ready to eat.

19

SNIFFING OUT

Many animals have a powerful sense of smell. They learn much more about what is going on around them through smell than people do.

The police use **dogs** to help them **find things** by smelling.

There are smells in the water as well as in the air. **Sharks** can **sniff out blood** in the water from a long way away.

Animals often have a **strong scent** so that they can smell each other.

It is easy for a baby deer to be separated from its mother in a big herd. The mother knows which one is her baby by its smell.

A **fox** marks out the area it lives and hunts in with **a strong smell** that warns other foxes to keep away!

✋ TRY IT OUT!

How good is your sense of smell? Peel an orange and put it on a plate. Ask a friend to hide it in a room. Can you find the orange just by using your sense of smell?

TASTE

Stick out your tongue and look at it in the mirror. Can you see little bumps on it? These are your taste buds. Your taste buds can taste things that are salty, sweet, sour or bitter.

What do the foods and drinks in the picture taste like – salty, sweet, sour or bitter?

Have you noticed that food doesn't have such a strong taste when you have a cold and can't smell very well?

Sometimes you can tell what's for dinner just by the **smell**. The food's smell makes it **taste more**.

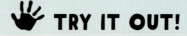 **TRY IT OUT!**

With an adult, hold you nose and shut your eyes while you eat a piece of cheese, then chocolate, then lemon and then some chicken. Can you tell what you are eating just by the taste? Now try without holding your nose. Does it taste better?

Animals use their sense of taste a lot as well. This **monkey** is feasting on sweet-tasting fruit.

This **caterpillar** is poisonous and has a nasty taste. A bird who has pecked it once learns never to eat this kind of caterpillar again.

Flying insects can taste with their feet! They know at once whether they have landed on something good to eat.

Snakes flicker their tongues and taste the air. This way they can tell if there is food or danger nearby.

THINK ABOUT IT!

What food do you like to taste. Do you like the smell as well? Can you think of some food that you like to taste but you don't like to smell?

KEEPING SAFE

Animals keep alert and use their senses all the time to warn them of danger. You use your five senses to look out for danger signals, too. You learn and remember them and this helps to keep you safe.

When you cross a road, you are told to 'stop, look and listen!'. You look both ways for traffic and you listen for the sound of cars as well, before you decide if it is safe to cross.

Your skin feels hot when you get too close to a radiator. You know not to touch it in case it burns you.

 **LOOK AGAIN!**

Look again at page 19. What danger signal does a bad smell give you?

Food that has gone off usually smells bad. You know it is not good to eat it. The food would probably taste nasty, too.

What do you think you might do if you had a mouthful?

THINK ABOUT IT!

Look at this cat. It is using its senses to work out if it has found something to eat, to play with or to be very careful of! When you go somewhere new or see something strange, think about how you are using your senses to find out about what is going on around you.

USEFUL WORDS

ANTENNAE
Some animals, such as snails and insects, have long, sensitive feelers on their heads called antennae. Antennae can be used to touch, smell, taste or hear.

BALANCE
To keep or put something in a steady position so it doesn't fall.

BRAIN
Your brain is inside your head. You think with your brain and use it to make sense of the world around you.

EARS
Ears are the part of your body that you hear with. The ear flaps on the side of your head collect sound. Inside your head are the parts of the ear that are sensitive to sound.

ENEMY
An enemy is someone who may do you harm. Animals that hunt are enemies of the animals they eat.

EYES
Your eyes are the part of your body that you see with. They are sensitive to light and colour.

GERMS
Germs carry diseases that can make you feel ill. Germs are too tiny to see.

HUNTER
Hunters are animals that catch and kill other animals for food.

INFORMATION

Information is anything that you can know. Information can be the facts you see on the television news. Your senses give you information about what is happening around you.

NOSE

Your nose is sensitive to smells in the air. You smell things when your breathe in through your nose.

PREY

Animals that are hunted and killed by other animals for food are called prey.

SCENT

A scent is a kind of smell. Many animals have a strong scent so that they can smell each other.

SENSES

Seeing, hearing, feeling, smelling and tasting are the five senses. You use your senses to tell you what is going on all around you.

SENSITIVE

Being sensitive means to be able to sense things. The parts of your body that you sense with are sensitive in different ways. For example, your skin is sensitive to touch and your nose is sensitive to smell.

SIGN LANGUAGE

People who cannot hear well use sign language. They use hand signs and body movements to talk to each other instead of sounds.

TASTE BUDS

Taste buds are the little bumps on your tongue that are sensitive to taste. They tell you if food or drink is sweet, salty, sour or bitter.

TONGUE

Your tongue is inside your mouth. You taste with your tongue.

WHISKERS

Whiskers are long, sensitive hairs that grow around the mouths of many animals. They help the animal to feel what is going on around them.

QUIZ

Now it's time to see how much you have learned. Try out this quick quiz to test your knowledge.

1 **What are the five senses?**

a) Seeing, hearing, feeling, smelling and tasting

b) Seeing, moving, resting, sleeping and laughing

c) Sleeping, hearing, dancing, eating and drinking

2 **What can cause us to see colours less clearly?**

a) The wind

b) The dark

c) Bright light

3 **Why do antelope have eyes on the sides of their head?**

a) So they can see all around and avoid danger

b) Because it looks nice

c) To match their ears

4 **What part of our body do we use to hear?**

a) Eyes

b) Nose

c) Ears

5 **Which area of skin on your hand is most sensitive to touch?**

a) Palm

b) Fingertips

c) Back of the hand

6) Which of these animals have whiskers to help them feel their way in the dark?

a) Snails
b) Butterflies
c) Mice

 7) What part of our body do we use to smell?

a) Nose
b) Ears
c) Eyes

 8) How do police dogs use their senses to help us find things?

a) Touching
b) Smelling
c) Tasting

 9) Where can you find your taste buds?

a) On your tongue
b) On your hand
c) On your ears

10) How do we use our senses to keep us safe when crossing a road?

a) Our skin feels hot
b) We smell a bad smell
c) We stop, look and listen

FURTHER INFORMATION

BOOKS TO READ

- *Science in Action: The Senses series* by Sally Hewitt (QED 2018)
- *Science is everywhere: Super Senses* by Rob Colson (Wayland 2018)
- *Human Body, Animal Bodies: Senses* by Izzi Howell (Wayland 2017)

WEBSITES TO VISIT

- **Head over to BBC Bitesize:** What are the senses? where you will find a useful video and quiz about this topic: https://www.bbc.co.uk/bitesize/topics/z9yycdm/articles/zxy987h
- **Visit Neuroscience for Kids:** Senses to find some amazing experiments about your senses: https://faculty.washington.edu/chudler/chsense.html

ATTRACTIONS TO EXPLORE

Explore the **Eden Project** in Cornwall and discover all the ways your senses help you to experience the natural world. Visit **Eureka! The National Children's Museum** in Halifax, Yorkshire, to explore interactive exhibits all about sound, sight and smell (and more!). Go to the **Glasgow Science Centre** and challenge your senses in their Question of Perception exhibit where nothing is quite as it seems!

NOTE TO PARENTS AND TEACHERS

Every effort has been made by the publisher to ensure that these websites contain no inappropriate or offensive material. However, because of the nature of the Internet, it is impossible to guarantee that the content of these sites will not be altered. We strongly advise that Internet access is supervised by a responsible adult.

ABOUT
THIS BOOK

Children are natural scientists. They learn by touching and feeling, noticing, asking questions and trying things out for themselves. The books in the *Get into Science!* series are designed for the way children learn. Familiar objects are used as starting points for further learning. *The Five Senses* starts with a child eating an orange and explores how the senses work.

Each double page spread introduces a new topic, such as skin. Information is given, questions asked and activities suggested that encourage children to make discoveries and develop new ideas for themselves. Look out for these panels throughout the book:

TRY IT OUT! indicates a simple activity, using safe materials, that proves or explores a point.

THINK ABOUT IT! indicates a question inspired by the information on the page but which points the reader to areas not covered by the book.

LOOK AGAIN introduces a cross-referencing activity that links themes and facts throughout the book.

Encourage children not to take the familiar world for granted. Point things out, ask questions and enjoy making scientific discoveries together.

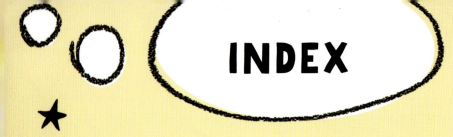

INDEX